She Takes Revenge (A Tale of Lies)
Jo Ann Atcheson Gray

Copyright © [2024] by [Jo Ann Atcheson Gray]

All rights reserved.

No portion of this book may be reproduced in any form without written permission from the publisher or author, except as permitted by U.S. copyright law.

Published by Jo Ann Gray

Contents

She Takes Revenge (A Tale of Lies)   1

She Takes Revenge (A Tale of Lies)   2

Fullpage image   25

She Takes Revenge (A Tale of Lies)

She Takes Revenge (A Tale of Lies)

Vivian. That's my name. I've always been a logical person, I never really believed in the supernatural, until I met a vampire...

I stood on the banks of the musky bayou, the weight of the Louisiana night pressing in around me. The air was thick with humidity, clinging to my darkened skin like a wet shroud, as if the swamps themselves were trying to pull me into their depths. The full moon, bright and haunting, hung low in the sky, casting a silvery glow over the twisted cypress trees, that loomed like sentinels in the dark. The dense canopy above me blocked out most of the starlight, leaving me with only the moon's cold light to guide me. I inhaled deeply, the scent of brackish water and decaying vegetation filling my lungs. The sounds of the mysterious bayou surrounded me, the croak of bullfrogs, the chirp of crickets, and the occasional splash of something large, like an alligator, moving beneath the murky waters, but it was the eerie silence that unnerved me the most. The way the sounds seemed to drop away whenever I stepped closer, deeper into the shadows, as if the swamp itself was holding its breath, waiting for my next move.

SHE TAKES REVENGE (A TALE OF LIES)

Two, long years had passed since my brother, Toby, had mysteriously vanished within the bayou, into this maze of water and darkness. Two years since he had walked into the heart of the bayou and never returned. We, the New Orleans police department, had searched for many weeks, many months, dredging the dirty waters of the swamps, combing through the dense underbrush, but we had found nothing, not even a small amount of any evidence of my older brother. No body, no sign of trouble or any struggles, just the empty silence that stretched on like a never-ending nightmare.

For the people of New Orleans, Toby's disappearance was just another ghost story being whispered among the locals, a tale to merely scare children away from the swamps, but for me, it was a wound that refused to heal, a question that haunted me every waking moment. The police investigators, eventually, ruled it as an unsolved disappearance, a possible drowning, just a simple individual consumed by the swamp itself, yet I refused to accept that. I refused to simply close the case completely, something inside me just could not accept the fact that my brother was eaten by an alligator or drowned in the uncaring waters of the bayou.

Now, I was back, standing at the very spot within the bayou, his home, where Toby had last been seen, my mind swirling with several unanswered questions and half-formed theories. After his memorial was held, I had dedicated my very life to solving the mysteries of this unsolved disappearance. I had uncovered many cases of others, their murders, their disappearances, but this one, this deeply personal case, just eluded me. As a mere woman of logic and reason, just a Creole woman, I refused to entertain the whispers of the supernatural that followed Toby's disappearance like a dark shadow, but the more I dug into the truth of it all, the more I found myself confronted with things I could not explain. I had been taught throughout my childhood about voodooism, curses, and many folklores about unseen forces that were unexplainable, yet I never really bothered to believe in such things. I was a simple, reasonable, petite woman, determined to prove what was right.

As I brushed a strand of my dark, black hair from my face, I tightened my firm grip on my flashlight, its beam cutting through the darkness. The swamp was a mere labyrinth of many shadows and hidden secrets, and I intended to uncover every one of these secrets to my brother's vanishing, even if it meant confronting the imagined monsters that his in the dark.

Over the two years, the investigation into Toby's disappearance had been a series of endless dead ends and many false leads. At first, the police investigators had assumed he was a mere victim of the bayou, as I already mentioned, that he had somehow gotten lost or fallen prey to an alligator. But when days turned into weeks, and weeks into months, without a single clue of evidence, the case had gone cold, being closed. I did not accept that; couldn't even begin to accept the fact that it was closed.

Toby was my eldest brother, my protector, the one who had always been there for me when our parents had passed away from an automobile accident, when we were only in adolescent years. He was the one person I had left in this vast world; I refuse to believe he was gone forever. If he was truly gone, deceased, I wanted to know why and I wanted to how, who took his life. When the police, the investigators, that I work with everyday had given up, I took matters into my own hands, using my skills as a detective to comb through the faint evidence, interviewing anyone, everyone, who might have seen or heard something about Toby, but every lead was turned to dust, every clue led further away, into a maze of mere confusion and despair. The residents of the bayou spoke of strange, evil creatures, of dark shadows that moved through the trees late at night, of eyes that glowed red, like embers all through the swamps. They spoke of the Rougarou, a werewolf-like creature that haunted the bayou, and other, older, evil things that had no names, no pulse.

I dismissed these tales as nothing but mere superstitions, but now, standing on the edge of the bayou with the moon casting long, eerie shadows over the still waters, I wondered if I had been too quick to judge. Something had taken my brother, something that left no trace, and if I had to wade through every ghost story and urban legend to find the truth, I would.

As I made my way deeper into the mystic, quiet bayou, the trees closed in around me, their gnarled branches reaching out like skeletal fingers. The path was uneven, the moist ground soft and treacherous beneath my boots. I moved cautiously, carefully, my flashlight sweeping over the twisted roots and mossy patches of swamp water that gleamed like dark mirrors in the night. Every so often, I would stop, just listening to the sounds of the night, trying to pick up on any hint of movement, strange movement, any sign that I was not alone out here, but the swamp was a master of much deception. Its sounds and shadows playing tricks on the mind, mind games that made one fearful. More than once, I found myself startled, turning, thinking I had seen something out of the corner of my eye, only to find that nothing was there. The deeper I went into the bayou, the more I felt a sense of great unease growing within me, a feeling that I was being watched by something. It was merely irrational; I knew that the simple product of too many sleepless nights and too many unanswered questions. But I knew, within my bones, that it was there, something like a cold, creeping sensation that sent shivers down my spine. And then, just as I was beginning to think that this trip to the bayou had been another dead end, I saw it, a faint glow in the distance, a small flicker of light that seemed to dance just beyond the edge of my vision. It was so faint, so fleeting, that I thought I might have imagined it, but there it was again, a flash of red, like a pair of flaming eyes watching me from the darkness.

My heart began to race fearfully, as I tightened my grip on the flashlight, moving cautiously toward the light, the red glow of what seemed like eyes. The ground became softer, moister, my boots sinking into the mud with every step, but I pushed on, driven by the need to know, to find some clue that would lead me to my brother. My determination was the only thing carrying me at this point. As I drew closer, the light seemed to move, flickering in and out of existence, leading me deeper into the heart of the bayou. I knew I should turn back, that I was walking into the dark unknown, But I could not stop myself, I had to keep going. It was as if I was being drawn by some invisible force, pulled toward a truth I was not yet ready to face. The light, still glowing like fire, led me to a small clearing, the trees parting, slightly, to reveal a pool of dirty water that gleamed like black glass in the moonlight, and there, standing on the edge of the pool of water, was a figure, a tall dark shadow of a man, a creature, its eyes glowing like twin embers of a fire in the night.

I froze, my heart pounding in my chest. The dark figure turned slowly, its reddened eyes locking onto mine, and for a brief moment, I felt a chill so deep it seemed to freeze my very soul. I wanted to run, to scream for help, to turn and flee back into the safety, the security of the trees, but my feet refused to retreat, I could not move. I was rooted to the very spot where I stood, caught in the gaze of the creature before me, with my flashlight held tightly in my grasp beaming straight into this creature's face. With my other hand resting firmly on my pistol attached to my side.

"Who are you?" I demanded, my voice trembling, yet brave, with a mixture of fear and defiance. "What do you want? What are you?"

The mysterious figure did not answer me, but I could feel its gaze piercing through me, as if it was looking not just at me, but inside me, seeing everything that I was, everything that I inwardly feared, and then, just as suddenly as it had appeared, the figure was gone, dissolving into the shadows like a wisp of smoke.

I stumbled back, my breath coming in ragged gasps, as the overall fear swept over me. I had seen many things, many criminals, in my time as a detective, but nothing like this figure, this creature with red eyes that I just saw. I knew, deep down, that I had just come face to face with something supernatural, something beyond the realm of anything natural, of anything reasonable, something that defied all logic and reason. But I also knew, with a certainty that burned in my chest, that this was the first real clue that I had found in two years. Whatever the creature was, it was connected to Toby's disappearance. I could feel it within, and I was going to find out how.

The next morning, the sun rose over the city of New Orleans, casting a golden light over the entire French Quarter, where the streets were already beginning to fill with tourists, the hustle and bustle of the day beginning, but I was not there to see it. I was in my small, cluttered apartment, surrounded by various maps, photos and stacks of notes, my mind still racing with the implications of what I had seen. O hadn't slept, couldn't sleep, not with the mere image of those red glowing eyes that were burned into my mind. I had spent the early hours of the morning going over every detail of my encounter from last night, trying to make some sense of it. Trying to fit it into some kind of rational framework, but there was nothing rational about what I had seen, nothing that could be explained by the laws of nature.

I was a logical Creole woman, a mere detective trained to see through any lies and any deception, but this was something else, something that defied everything I had ever believed in, and yet, I could not deny what I had actually seen, what I had actually witnessed with my own eyes. I couldn't deny the cold, hard truth, reality, that was staring me straight in the face. There was something in that bayou, something evil, something that had taken my brother, and it was still out there, watching, waiting, but I wasn't going to be afraid. I was determined that I was going to find it, whatever it was, and I was going to get some answers. For my brother, Toby, for myself, and for the peace that eluded me for so long now, I would find justice, my closure. But what I had not come to realize was that the actual truth I sought would bring me face to face with a darkness that would change me forever, a darkness that wore the face of a man, a vampire named Antonio, an immortal being with many secrets of his own, secrets that would bind us together in a web of mere lies, betrayal, and a brief love that was as dangerous as it was forbidden. I was about to embark on a journey that would take me deep into the heart of the darkness, into a world where evil creatures, mere monsters, were actually real, and the fine line between hunter and prey was not always so clear. I would have to decide, make a hard choice, what I was willing to sacrifice for the truth, and for a love that defied everything I had ever known. The love for my missing brother, Toby; was I ready, willing to lose my own life in finding the truth of Toby's disappearance?

My investigation had led me deep into the heart of the city's underbelly, the bayou, the swamps, where many untold secrets festered, and many dangers lurked in the dirty, dark waters. It was there where I had first encountered my supernatural sighting, a gathering of odd, mesmerizing, yet frightful emotions still swirled inside in as I pondered on those red eyes.

search of this vampire, he was waiting for me at the little table inside the rugged shed.

I found myself getting entangled with Antonio, drawn to him despite my better judgement. He told me many stories of his past, his world, that he was centuries old and had seen many things, yet he did not mention Toby at all. I wondered if it all was just lies wrapped in a seducing charm. Each time I tried to bring up my brother, Antonio would deflect, his smile never faltering, as he would continue speaking about some other past tale. But in my heart, I knew he was hiding something, hiding some kind of truth about Toby. My thoughts seemed like nightmares, at times, as I listened to this creature speak, visions of my brother flashed in my mind, as if he were tangled in darkness, his mere voice calling for anyone to help him. I couldn't shake the feeling that Antonio was somehow involved in the murder of my brother.

After relentless listening to all his estranged tales of his past, his sorrows, his past lovers, he finally mentioned Toby. This vampire let it slip that he was there the night Toby was in the swamp trying to capture an alligator near his place of dwelling. I gasped when Antonio said those words. So, this creature finally quit playing with me, finally quit telling me lies, and admitted that he was there, with Toby, that night. Confronting him with next words was like stepping into a massive storm, "You killed him. You killed my brother that night, didn't you?" I accused, my voice barely above a whisper, fear mingling with fury, with rage.

"Vivian, it was never meant to be..." he began, but I cut him off, as I stood, enraged within myself, with much pain and hurt at the actual thought of Toby being dead.

"Don't. Just don't speak anymore! You are a monster!" I screamed as I tried to make my way to the door to go for help.

His eyes flashed red, with something unreadable, as I darted past him, knowing that he had allowed me to leave, "I'm sorry, Vivian. I told you the truth was dangerous."

Torn between wanting to kill this creature and being drawn to his mesmerizing allure, and the mere memory of my brother, I faced a profound inner struggle. I did not want to feel any kind of affection for this vampire, not after the mere thought that he, possibly, had murdered Toby. Yet, his magnetic pull seemed too undeniable, too alluring, too strong, as if it was awakening deep, inner feelings I had long ago buried.

In the dead of the night, I turned around, determined, I would end this creature. I did not need any help; I could handle it. The case was already closed anyway, so, I needed to end this myself. Entering the small dwelling again, I boldly confronted Antonio, as he stood next to the small table, as if he knew that I was returning. He smiled, evilly, as I entered. Holding a sharp stick, in the shape of a small wooden stake that was made of the cypress trees in the bayou, and my pistol in my hands, I came ready for a fight.

"This is for murdering my brother," I declared, the weight of the world resting on my shoulders, as I bolted through the fragile wooden door with my gun aimed straight at Antonio.

His expression shifted, as he laughed a small chuckle, sorrow and a shadowed rage across his countenance, "You think you can simply defeat me, Vivian? I am beyond death."

I fired my pistol straight into his chest, unloading every bullet. The bayou became our battleground, thick fog settled, swirling all around us, as this creature lunged at me, time seemed to freeze as I dropped my gun to the moist ground just outside the little shed's entrance. I fought with all I had, not just for Toby, but for myself. Each move I made felt like an echo of my brother's spirit guiding me. In a final, desperate thrust, I plunged the sharp wooden stick, this makeshift stake, deep into his undead heart. Antonio's red eyes widened, a mixture of pain and regret etched upon his pale face. "Vivian... forgive me..."

As he crumpled to the mossy grass on the ground at my feet, shadows seemed to recede, leaving behind the mere stillness of the night. I felt an overwhelming sadness wash over, like I had taken the life of a loved one. It was over, but at what cost?

Days passed before I could actually return to the bayou. I had to go and clean out my brother's house that rested in the heart of the swamp. I stood alone, the weight of my choice heavy on my heart. The truth was still not exactly clear as to what actually happened to my brother, but it left scars that would never heal. I had avenged Toby, yet I had lost a part of myself in the process. As I walked away from the dwelling where my brother had lived for years, the moon hung high, casting silver light over the dark waters that had once concealed so many secrets. I returned to the French Quarter as I ventured to my apartment. The city was alive and many stories still was told of Antonio, the vampire, the dark lord. Though I had killed my brother's murderer, the closure just was not there. The mere shadows of love and loss still lingered, shaping me into something of confusion.

In New Orleans, the line between love and hatred was as murky as the dirty waters of the bayou, I knew I would forever be its detective, always unraveling the mysterious, tangled threads of the city's mere heart. Months passed after that encounter with Antonio in the bayou that night, yet I was still bothered within myself about the truth to Toby's death. I just couldn't get the closure that should have been there. After restless curiosities, I kept investigating the myths about Antonio, I just couldn't get him out of my mind.

One late night, after an investigation of a mysterious murder within the Quarter near Royal Street, I was walking back to my apartment.

As I turned the corner of Royal Street, I discovered that Antonio was still alive, still existing. When his eyes met mine, he hastily vanished. I was furious, confused.

I went back to the bayou, deep within the swamps, only to find that Antonio was not there. The shed was no more. it was only a pile of ashes now. Scanning the darkness of the swamp with my flashlight, I searched for any signs of Antonio. Finally, I felt a presence ease up behind me, I knew it was him...

The air was heavy with the thick scent of rain-soaked earth as I stood over Antonio, the vampire who had haunted my every waking thought for months now. We were deep in the heart of the swampy bayou, far from the lights and noise of New Orleans. The moon hung low in the sky, casting a silvery, haunting glow over the twisted branches of the weeping cypress trees. The bayou seemed to hold its breath, as if the whole world was waiting for what would happen next. Antonio was on his knees, his hands bound behind him with iron shackles that burned his skin. I had prepared for this encounter, this time, as I gathered all my necessary defense items to take this creature down for good. Before actually coming back to the dark bayou, I went the day after the night in Quarter, when I realized he still existed, and prepared myself for this fight. His once-pristine shirt was badly torn and bloodied by my blood, clinging to his pale chest like a second skin. Antonio had severely attacked me while my back was turned, but I was ready. I unloaded my pistol on him, sinking all the silver bullets into his chest as he, brutally, gripped me by my neck, cutting my breath off. His sharp, yet deadly fingernails sinking into my flesh. The silver bullets quickly weakened his tight grip as he tumbled to the moist grass, letting me regain my breath. I gasped as I jumped hastily to my feet, overtaking Antonio in his weakened condition. His dark, hollow red eyes seemed to dim their glow, eyes that once seemed to captivate me with their impossible depth, were now extremely dull with exhaustion and slight pain. Even in this moment of defeat, there was a flicker of something defiant in his weakened gaze, a small spark of the predator that he truly was.

I held a sacred, golden dagger in my hand that I had come across in the alleyways of the French Quarter, a little shop that was full of ancient relics. This was where I retrieved all the items that I needed to fight against a vampire. The mere blade of this golden dagger glistened in the moonlight. This was no ordinary weapon; it was a sacred object, an ancient artifact that I had unearthed during my visit to the little shop, the old lady with too much jewelry that worked there, told me of an old tale, of whispers throughout the Quarter. The legend was 'In New Orleans, it is said that the only way to properly put your demons to permanent rest, is to kill it with gold, straight through its heart.' This blade was meant to take an immortal's life, it was fashioned by an old, Creole, voodoo priestess many centuries ago. So, the woman in the little shop, graciously allowed me to borrow this dagger merely on promises that I would return it. I told her the whole story of Antonio and the death of my brother, and she actually believed me, understood my problem.

Antonio only watched me with a bitter, cruel smile, and a small, faint hollow laugh escaping his pale lips as he saw the determination etched in my features. "So, this is how it all ends," he said, his voice a rough whisper, "After everything, after I kindly allowed you to live, you have come to kill me with pure gold. How poetic, Vivian."

My hand trembled slightly as I held the ancient blade, my heart pounding in my chest, only the full moon above lighting the bayou. I had waited so long for this actual moment, had fought so hard to get here. This man, this vampire, this predator, had taken my brother, Toby, from me, had lied to me, had deceived me, had twisted my mind, my heart, in strange ways that I could hardly comprehend, but there was still something in his eyes that held me back, something that made me hesitate.

"Tell me why," I demanded, my voice cold and steady despite the storm raging inside me. "Tell me the full truth before I end this, before I end you. Why did you take Toby? Why did you allow me to be pulled into your twisted world?"

Antonio's gaze softened, his expression shifting from one of mere mockery to something far more vulnerable, almost human. He drew in a slow breath, as if savoring the taste of the night air one last time, "You want the truth, Vivian?" he asked, his voice low, almost apologetic. "I did not want to hurt you further with the true tale of your brother. You fully believe that knowing the truth will actually bring you peace?"

I did not respond, I only stared a deadly stare at him, as I held my grip tighter on the gold dagger, and Antonio seemed to take that as his cue to continue... "In New Orleans, it is said that the only way to put your demons to rest is to kill them with gold, pure gold." he began, his hollow eyes locking onto mine, a strange, haunting flicker in their depths, "But what no one tells you is that sometimes... those demons are the very thing keeping you alive."

He paused, the silence stretching between us like a taut wire. When he spoke again, his mere voice was softer, tinged with a slight pain that I had never seen in him before now. " I did not actually kill your brother, Vivian. Not in the brutal way you think. He came to me... seeking a cure for something he could not name, a darkness that was eating at him, eating him from the inside. He was lost, haunted by his own demons far worse than anything I could ever be. Toby, your brother, was already an immortal, turned by an immature vampire somewhere within the Quarter on late night, while he was in a bar. He came to me for help, he sought me out by tempting me with human blood, blood he spilled by taking many lives within New Orleans. He was a mere monster, same as I, yet he wanted to end his tortuous nature. So, I told him how to do it. I bound him with chains to one of these very cypress trees, as I left him there for the sun to consume him. I did him an honor, Vivian."

I felt the ground shift beneath me, as if the very fabric of my reality was unraveling, "Liar!" I shouted, shaking my head in disagreement, refusing to actually believe Antonio's words. "No. You took him. It was you, wasn't it? You turned him into one of your kind. I know exactly what you are, Antonio."

He let out a hollow laugh, his head tilting back as if he found some dark humor in her accusation. "No, Vivian. If only it were that simple. Your brother... he wanted to escape the pain, the guilt, the mere memories that tormented him. I simply offered him a way out, a choice, but he became afraid as I chained him to the tree. He started to refuse my help, but I convinced him, with force, to choose death over his damnation of eternity. I only helped him find peace, a release in his tortured soul."

The words from Antonio hung in the air, each one like a knife slicing through my heart. My vision blurred with warm tears that I refused to shed, my mind reeling with the implications. 'Was this just another one of Antonio's mockeries, one of his lies, a last lash at attempting to hurt me, or save himself? Or was there a grain of truth buried in his confession?'

"Why should I believe you, believe anything you just told me?" I asked, demanding, my voice breaking with pain, with anger, as the blade trembled in my grasp. "After everything, why should I trust you, your lies, your mockery, it was all to deceive me, wasn't it? You killed my brother for your own selfish desires, your own bloodlust, didn't you?"

I wanted to hear the words from Antonio, I wanted him to confess that he was merely telling me lies, but his hollow, dull eyes seemed so sincere. As Antonio's expression softened, weakened, for a moment, he merely looked almost human, almost... regretful. "Because I have nothing left in my immortal life, nothing of any value to protect," he simply said, "Because I am tired, Vivian. Tired of this mere existence, tired of the endless nights and the intense blood hunger that never truly fades or is ever truly satisfied. I have lived too long, many centuries, lost too many lovers, and if tonight is the night I meet my end, then so be it. You deserve to know the truth, Vivian, even if it damns me."

Antonio slowly bowed his head, exposing the pale column of his throat, offering me the final blow, "Do it, Vivian. Kill me with you ancient, golden blade and put your inner demons to rest, but know this, I did take Toby's immortal life. I gave him what he had asked me for... simply a way out. I removed his head from his undead shoulders as I pierced his heart with a silver knife, leaving him there for the sun to consume him to mere ashes."

My hands shook with rage, anger, the weight of the gold dagger growing heavier with each second that passed. Everything I had ever believed, everything I had ever fought for, was crumbling around me, as I replayed his final words to me in my mind. The need for vengeance, the pure anger that had driven me this far, was all faltering in the face of this broken creature of the night who was patiently kneeling before me, waiting for his fate.

The bayou was silent apart from the faint sounds of the massive group of crickets that loomed in the distance, and the soft rustle of the wind through the trees. With warm tears streaming down my face, I cried out, a scream that even an owl would be frightened of, "It's over now!"

With half rage and half sorrow, I plunged the ancient relic, the golden dagger deep into Antonio's chest, piercing his heart. He gasped, his hollow eyes no longer glowing red, as they widened in a state of mere shock, but there was no hatred in them, his mere gaze was only a deep, abiding sadness. His undead body shuddered, the life draining from him in a rush of mere darkness, and for a brief moment, I thought I saw something like relief in his eyes, a release from the torment of centuries that had bound him. As his body crumbled to the mossy grass, the mere truth of his final confession hung in the air, lingering like the mist over the bayou. I fell to my knees, the golden dagger slipping from my fingers, the weight of my actions crashing down upon me. I had killed the monster who took my brother's life, whether it was mortal or immortal, but in doing so, I had also killed any curiosity, any boldness that I had left within me.

The moon dipped below the horizon, the bayou returning to its eternal silence, but for me, the questions of Antonio's confession remained, gnawing at my soul like the very demons that Antonio had spoken of... 'Was Antonio really an evil being? Did he actually take Toby's life, immortal or not? Why would he lie to me about he first confession that he had spoken of?'

I thought on the phrase, 'The only way to put your demons to rest was to kill them with gold,' but what if that actual demon, that mere vampire, you killed, was the only one who saved you from yourself? What if he actually was that one demon to save Toby from himself? What if Antonio was the one who really did my brother an act of kindness by ending his immortal life, his torment?

Shaking these haunting thoughts from my mind, I rested on the fact that I ended this mystery, this case of my brother's disappearance.

I avenged his killer, whether it was wrong or not, or whether it was simply an act of kindness, it was now over. Toby's death could be peaceful now, I had found my closure.

As the first light of dawn broke over the swamp, the sun rose brightly, I stood alone, the shattered pieces of my world scattered around me like so many shards of broken glass. I had my vengeance, but at what cost? I could never see my brother Toby again now. In the depths of the bayou, where the shadows never truly sleep, the faint echoes of Antonio's final words, his final confession, a haunting whisper that would follow me for the rest of my days, as his body quickly dissolved into ashes from the glowing rays of the sun above, blowing away through the swampy bayou of New Orleans.

The End.

Milton Keynes UK
Ingram Content Group UK Ltd.
UKHW020915291124
451807UK00013B/939